Published by Creative Education and
Creative Paperbacks
P.O. Box 227, Mankato, Minnesota 56002
Creative Education and Creative Paperbacks
are imprints of The Creative Company
www.thecreativecompany.us

Design by The Design Lab
Production by Chelsey Luther
Printed in the United States of America

Photographs by Dreamstime (Isselee, Cathy Keifer),
Getty Images (Deborah Rust), Shutterstock (Evgeniy
Ayupov, bierchen, Melissa Brandes, Ersler Dmitry,
Eric Isselee, Rozi Kassim, Cathy Keifer), SuperStock
(Biosphoto, FLPA, NHPA, PhotoStock-Israel/age
fotostock)

Library of Congress Cataloging-in-Publication Data
Riggs, Kate.
Geckos / Kate Riggs.
p. cm. — (Amazing animals)
Summary: A basic exploration of the appearance,
behavior, and habitat of geckos, the colorful climbing
lizards. Also included is a story from folklore explain-
ing how geckos became Hawaiian good-luck charms.
Includes index.
ISBN 978-1-60818-489-7 (hardcover)
ISBN 978-1-62832-089-3 (pbk)
1. Geckos—Juvenile literature. I. Title. II. Series:
Amazing animals.
QL666.L245R54 2015
597.95'2—dc23   2013051249

CCSS: RI.1.1, 2, 4, 5, 6, 7; RI.2.2, 5, 6, 7, 10;
RI.3.1, 5, 7, 8; RF.1.1, 3, 4; RF.2.3, 4

First Edition
9 8 7 6 5 4 3 2 1

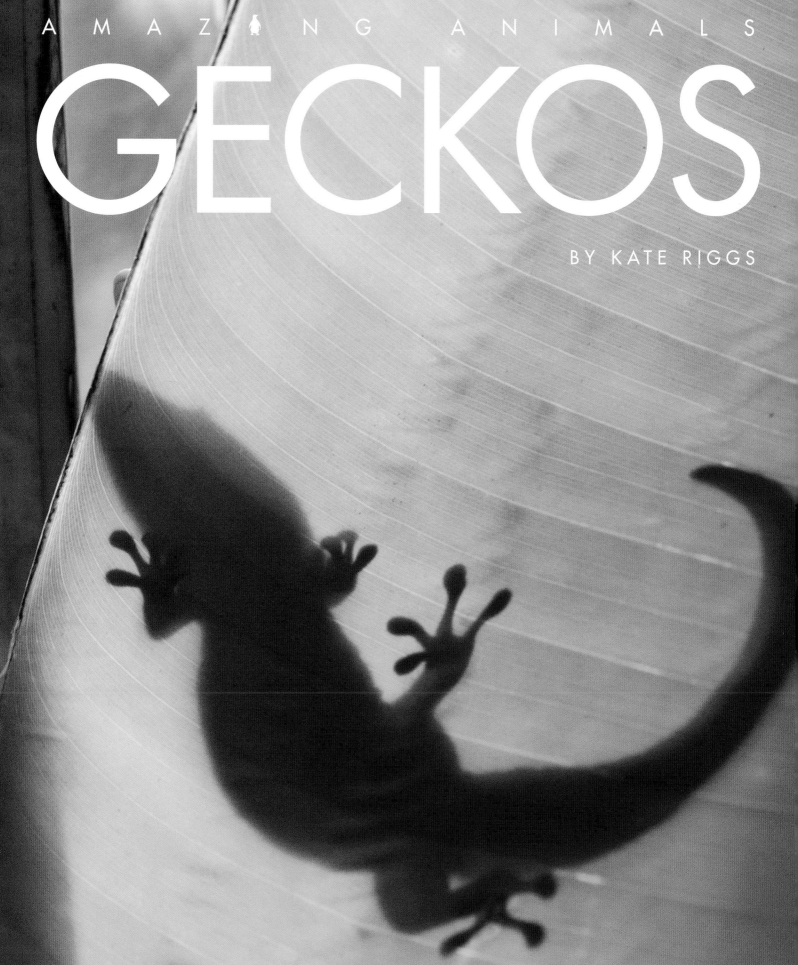

AMAZING ANIMALS

GECKOS

BY KATE RIGGS

CREATIVE EDUCATION • CREATIVE PAPERBACKS

*Eight kinds of geckos
live on the islands of
Hawaii*

Lizards called geckos live in warm places around the world. They are found on all **continents** except Antarctica. Some lizards hiss, but geckos make sounds such as chirping or barking.

continents Earth's seven big pieces of land

Some geckos lick water from their eyes to get moisture

Only 18 kinds of geckos have eyelids. Other geckos have a clear covering over their eyes. They lick their eyes to keep them clean. A gecko has a tail that can break off from the body. Sometimes a gecko will break off its tail to get away from **predators**.

predators animals that kill and eat other animals

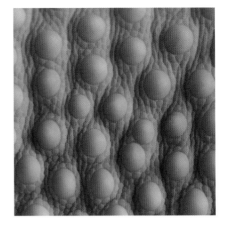

Geckos can be as small as 0.6 inch (1.6 cm). Giant day geckos can be 10 inches (25 cm) long. The most colorful geckos are active in daytime. Geckos have different markings on their skin. They come in many colors.

A gecko's small, rounded scales make its skin bumpy

Mossy leaf-tailed geckos (left) hide in plain sight

Geckos have pads on the bottoms of their toes. The sticky pads help geckos climb. Geckos can live in dry lands, rainy forests, and on **mountains**. Some geckos blend in with the sand, rocks, or trees around them.

mountains very big hills made of rock

Geckos eat insects and other small creatures. Larger geckos can eat small birds and **reptiles**. Geckos hunt for food in trees or on the ground. Some geckos eat fruit.

reptiles animals that have scales and a body that is always as warm or as cold as the air around it

Many geckos grow in their eggs for 6 to 12 weeks

A female gecko lays one or two eggs in leaves and bark. The **hatchlings** grow up on their own. Geckos live by themselves for about 6 to 10 years. Some kinds of geckos can live for 20 years in the wild.

hatchlings baby geckos

Geckos shed their skin every two to four weeks. They hide from predators like snakes and birds. They scream or chirp at other geckos that get too close. Geckos spend a lot of time hunting for food.

Reptiles like geckos grow larger bodies by shedding skin

Most geckos look for food at night. These geckos rest during the day. Geckos warm their bodies in the sun. They move to the shade when they get too hot.

Even geckos active at night may warm up in the sun

Many people keep geckos as pets. Leopard geckos are popular pets. People who live in the warmest parts of the world may see wild geckos. It can be fun to search for these noisy lizards!

Leaf-tailed geckos can spring from branch to branch

A Gecko Story

Do geckos bring good luck? People in Hawaii have believed this for a long time. They told a story about a gecko with a loud laugh that saved a king's daughter from danger. The king made the gecko guardian angel over all the Hawaiian Islands. Hawaiians still welcome geckos into their houses for good luck.

Read More

Arnosky, Jim. *All about Lizards*. New York: Scholastic Paperbacks, 2004.

Marsh, Laura. *Lizards*. Washington, D.C.: National Geographic, 2012.

Websites

National Geographic Kids: Gecko
http://kids.nationalgeographic.com/animals/gecko.html
Learn more about geckos and where they live.

Wild Kratts: All About Lizards Activity
http://www.pbs.org/parents/wildkratts/activities/all-about-lizards/
Learn more about how geckos climb by doing an experiment.

Note: Every effort has been made to ensure that the websites listed above are suitable for children, that they have educational value, and that they contain no inappropriate material. However, because of the nature of the Internet, it is impossible to guarantee that these sites will remain active indefinitely or that their contents will not be altered.